WOMEN Who LEAD

STORIES OF IMPACT AND INFLUENCE OF FEMALE LEADERS

DR. PAULETTE HARPER

THY WORD PUBLISHING

Published by Thy Word Publishing
Antioch, CA 94531

© 2024 Dr. Paulette Harper

Book Cover Design: Tyora Moody
Interior Book Design & Formatting: https://tywebbincreations.com
Editor: Niki Banning http://nikibvirtualservices.com/

Self-Publishing Coach: Dr. Paulette Harper Visit https://pauletteharper.com/services/ to access information about writing your own book.

All rights reserved. No part of this book may be used or reproduced, stored in or introduced into a retrieval system, or transmitted in any form including, photocopying, electronic or mechanical, recording or by any means without the express written consent from the author.

Scripture quotations marked "KJV" are taken from the Holy Bible, King James Version, Cambridge, 1769. Used by permission.

Scriptures marked AMP are taken from the AMPLIFIED BIBLE (AMP): Scripture taken from the AMPLIFIED® BIBLE, Copyright © 1954, 1958, 1962, 1964, 1965, 1987 by the Lockman Foundation Used by Permission. (www.Lockman.org)

Scriptures marked NIV are taken from the NEW INTERNATIONAL VERSION (NIV): Scripture taken from THE HOLY BIBLE, NEW INTERNATIONAL VERSION ®. Copyright© 1973, 1978, 1984, 2011 by Biblica, Inc.TM. Used by permission of Zondervan

Library of Congress Cataloging-in-Publication Data

Paperback: ISBN: 979-8-218-54728-8
Published and printed in the United States of America.

Contents

Acknowledgement	V
Sponsors	VII
Introduction	IX
1. Shattering Ceilings: The Power of a Woman Called to Preach Dr. Paulette Harper	1
2. My Transformational Leadership Journey Dr. Theresa A. Moseley	13
3. Empowered to Lead and Live: My Aunt's Legacy in My Leadership Cherise Buchanan	25
4. From Home to the C-Suite: How Networking Drove Success Susana Sarvis	38
5. Empowered to Rise: Unlocking the Strength to Overcome and Thrive Elizabeth Meigs	50

6. From Trials to Triumph: My Journey of Resilience and Leadership Dawn Stone	62
7. Leading with God, Passion, and Purpose Dr. Iris Wright	75
8. The Whisper of Faith: From Desert to Destiny Kristina S. Shauntee	84
Calling All Readers!	96
Other Books By	98
Write A Book With Me	100
Author Coaching Services	103

Acknowledgement

I want to extend my deepest gratitude to the remarkable individuals who have contributed to the realization of this book. Above all, I offer my deepest thanks to my Lord and Savior Jesus Christ, whose unwavering presence and guidance have been my constant source of strength throughout this transformative journey.

You are truly an incredible God!

To my friends and esteemed colleagues, your priceless feedback, profound insights, and unwavering encouragement have played an indispensable role in shaping my ideas and refining my writing.

A special acknowledgement to the extraordinary co-authors who entrusted me with their stories and allowed me to guide them through this extraordinary expedition. Your voices are powerful, and together, we are creating lasting impact.

Lastly, I want to express my heartfelt appreciation to the readers of this book. Your curiosity and unwavering support have been the driving force behind its inception. It is my sincere aspiration that *Women Who Lead* will illuminate and inspire all who delve into its pages.

I extend my heartfelt gratitude to each and every one of you for your invaluable contributions and unwavering support.

Visit https://www.onestoryuniversity.com/threesimplesteps to access a free resource to help you start writing your bestseller.

With gratitude,
Visionary Author
Dr. Paulette Harper
www.pauletteharper.com

WOMAN WHO LEAD

Stories of Impact and Influence of Female Leaders

We sincerely appreciate your sponsorship of *Women Who Lead*. Your support has been vital in empowering women and advancing our mission to positively impact lives. Thank you for purchasing a copy of our book and being a part of this important journey.

Alycia Singletary
Andrea Mayberry
Amie Archbold
Annie Hicks, Dr
Audrey Calery
Amy Miller

Brittany Crudupt
Bella Solis
Brenda Mayaka
Brianna Ward
Brittnie Watkins, Dr
Bonnie Rencher
Barbara Wright

Casey Fairley
Carl Inman
Carolyn Ballard
Cyrisse Allen

Dawon Sharp
Deborah Horn
Dwayne Kelly
Debra Meigs
Dan Bryant

Felicia Mares

Gus Singleton Jr., Dr
Grant Olbrich

Heather Schmidt

Ivan Lee
Ivery Daniels

Jacqueline Davis
Jaime Nelson
James Dorsey Sr.
Janice Love
Jasmine Welch
Jennie Johnson
Jessie Robinson
Judy Warren
Jacqueline Crider
Jan Dannels

Keith Shauntee
Karin Whittler
Kathleen Slawson
Kyra Wallace
Kathleen Bakken
Keri Bentsen
Kathy Williams

WOMAN WHO LEAD

Stories of Impact and Influence of Female Leaders

We sincerely appreciate your sponsorship of *Women Who Lead*. Your support has been vital in empowering women and advancing our mission to positively impact lives. Thank you for purchasing a copy of our book and being a part of this important journey.

Lakeea Kelly
Larry Guy
LaSondra Barnes, Dr
LaTisha Glass, Dr
Linda Meeder
Lauren Greene
Lisa Bradley
Linda Rogers
Lacy Shaffer

Martila Sanders
Melissa Durden
Michael Glass, Dr
Monica Houston
Melissa Daniell

Nakita Hale

Pam Hines
Pamela Allen
Pamela Lue-Hing
Patricia Hood
Paulette Pulley
Phoenix Asifa

Regina Leveston
Roland Sunkin III
Rodna Joseph

Samantha DeLoache
Sara LaCroix
Shantina Williams
Siobhan Saulsbury
Stan Parker, Dr., and Charlotte Parker, Faith Fellowship Baptist Church
Susana Briscoe-Alba
Sharon Bauer

Tina Lee
Tracshell Noble
Tracy Graham
Tony Grisham

Vickie Bridgewater

Yvonne Powell

Introduction

A Message from the Visionary Author Dr. Paulette Harper

Fifteen-Times Best-Selling Author | Speaker | Pastor | Nonfiction Self-Publishing Coach

Women Who Lead is a testament to the strength, resilience, and undeniable power of women who have chosen to step into leadership with purpose, passion, and faith. This book is not just a collection of stories; it is a movement—a rallying cry for women across the world to recognize their potential, embrace their divine calling, and lead with unwavering courage.

The women in this book come from diverse backgrounds, but they share a common thread: each has walked through trials, overcome obstacles, and risen to a place of influence by the grace of God. Their stories serve as powerful examples of what is possible when faith meets action, and when determination is fueled by a desire to not only succeed but to serve and uplift others.

As women of faith, we often find ourselves balancing multiple roles: as leaders in our homes, communities, businesses, and ministries. We carry the weight of expectations, not just from others, but from ourselves. Yet, it is in these challenges that we discover our strength. We find that leadership is not about having all the answers, but about trusting the One who does. It is about leading with grace, humility, and boldness, knowing that we are empowered by God to fulfill the assignments He has given us.

This book is for every woman who has ever questioned her worth or doubted her ability to lead. It is for those who have felt the nudge to step forward but hesitated, unsure of what the future might hold. Let the stories in Women Who Lead remind you that you are not alone. You are part of a sisterhood of women who have been called to lead, and through their experiences, you will find the inspiration, encouragement, and tools you need to rise to the challenge.

As you journey through the pages of this book, may you be empowered to step boldly into your calling, knowing that God has equipped you with everything you need to lead with excellence. You are a woman who leads, and the world is waiting for the impact only you can make.

With grace and gratitude,

Dr. Paulette Harper
Visit https://pauletteharper.com/signaturestoryworkbook/ to access a free recourse for aspiring authors.

Shattering Ceilings: The Power of a Woman Called to Preach

Dr. Paulette Harper

Upon surrendering my heart to the Lord, I sensed a profound "call" into ministry. At the time, my understanding of this calling was simply to serve, though I wasn't yet clear on how to do so. I was eager to please God, yet unsure of the path He had set before me. As I continued seeking His guidance, I soon realized that God had a deeper purpose for my life—one that went beyond acts of service. He was calling me to be a messenger of His Word, a preacher of the Gospel, entrusted with the mission of leading others to Him.

As I leaned into my time of prayer and devotion, God began to reveal His plan for me. The scripture from Matthew 28:19-20 became a guiding light for my journey with Christ, illuminating the responsibility that came with this calling:

Matthew 28:19-20 (NIV): "Therefore go and make disciples of all nations, baptizing them in the name of the Father and of the Son and of the Holy Spirit, and teaching them to obey everything I have commanded you. And surely I am with you always, to the very end of the age."

This passage brought clarity and purpose to my walk with God. I understood my calling wasn't just about proclaiming the Gospel but also about discipling others, nurturing their faith, and guiding them toward a deeper relationship with Christ. It became clear that my life was no longer my own—it was a vessel through which God would reach, heal, and transform lives. His promise to be with me always gave me the strength and courage to answer His call with confidence and humility.

At that time, my husband was also called into ministry, and we were led to serve together. The church where we both found salvation was a Baptist church, where the role of women in ministry was not as widely accepted—especially by the pastor. In those days, it was more common and acceptable for men to be called to preach, while women were typically encouraged to serve in other capacities, such as teaching children's church, working the altar, or leading Sunday school. While my early foundation as a believer involved all those roles, I felt a deep, undeniable yearning to preach.

Our church was just beginning to embrace a more progressive approach to worship. We were being introduced to the Holy Spirit's power, including the evidence of speaking in tongues. Yet despite this spiritual growth, the acceptance of women preachers still lagged behind. I distinctly remember when my husband and I had to sit down with the pastor to discuss our individual callings. It was clear from our conversation that he did not fully embrace the idea that God had placed a divine call on my life to preach His Word.

During that challenging season, I found great comfort in Ephesians 4:11-16, which reaffirmed what God had placed in my heart:

Ephesians 4:11-16 (KJV): "And he gave some, apostles; and some, prophets; and some, evangelists; and some, pastors and teachers; for the perfecting of the saints, for the work of the ministry, for the edifying of the body of Christ: till we all come in the unity of the faith, and of the knowledge of the Son of God, unto a perfect man, unto the measure of the stature of the fulness of Christ."

This scripture reminded me that God calls people according to His will, not based on societal norms or gender. I understood God shows no favoritism; His calling is not limited by human expectations. Even in the face of resistance, I knew with certainty that God had chosen me to preach His Word, and I had to trust His plan over the opinions of others.

I was fortunate to be encouraged by other women in the church who also felt called into ministry. They urged me not to be discouraged by the opposition but to continually seek God's guidance, trusting that, in time, He would open the eyes of others to the calling He had placed on my life. Their support was crucial during those early days, and it gave me the strength to stand firm, even when it seemed no one else understood. I held onto my faith, knowing God's plan would unfold in His timing. Slowly but surely, the pastor began to see what I had known all along—God had indeed called me to preach His Word.

After years of prayer, training, and devotion, my husband and I were called into the role of pastors. This new chapter in our lives was exciting–but it also brought a deep sense of responsibility. No amount of formal training or reading the best books on pastorship could fully prepare us for the reality of leading God's people. Stepping into pastoral leadership wasn't just about knowledge; it was about learning through real experiences, facing trials head-on, and overcoming adversity.

Pastoring is a unique journey that no book or course can truly prepare you for. It's an ongoing process of growth, where every situation and challenge teaches you more about the heart of ministry. From dealing with people's personal struggles to navigating church dynamics and spiritual warfare, each day brought new lessons. Some days, the weight of the role felt overwhelming—ministering to people's spiritual, emotional, and physical needs was not something to take lightly.

The truth is, pastoring is less about being perfect or having all the answers, and more about being available to God and His people. You learn to walk in humility, trusting God to give you wisdom and strength for each new challenge. The journey is filled with trials, but through them, you develop a deeper compassion for those you serve. There were moments of uncertainty, where my husband and I had to lean solely on our faith in God's promises, trusting Him to guide us through the storms.

The years we spent as pastors brought us face-to-face with the realities of ministry—brokenness, heartache, and sometimes opposition. But it also brought us immense joy, witnessing lives transformed by the power of God's Word. We learned that ministry isn't about having control or all the right answers; it's about surrendering to God's will, allowing Him to use us as vessels of His grace and truth.

The challenges shaped us, not just as leaders, but as people of faith. Through the trials and tests, we became stronger in our walk with Christ. Each struggle refined us, teaching us resilience, patience, and a deeper understanding of God's heart for His people. What we thought was preparation for ministry was just the beginning. The real preparation came through walking out our calling, facing adversity, and relying on God's unshakable faithfulness through it all.

Looking back, I realize that those experiences, as difficult as they were, equipped us for a greater purpose. It was through the trials that we learned how to truly pastor—by listening, serving, and loving our congregation through every season of life. And even when nothing seemed to prepare us for what was to come, God was always there, shaping us for the ministry He had designed just for us. Despite the hardships, I knew that God had placed us in this position for a purpose, and it was through these trials that we would grow into the pastors He had called us to be.

But then, the unexpected happened.

Our marriage unraveled. We got divorced. It was, without a doubt, the hardest season of my life. I often found myself wondering how I could ever recover from such devastation—how I could heal from the heartbreak and find a way to live again, now alone. Twenty-three years of marriage were gone. Just. Like. That.

I realized God had all the while prepared me for this moment—I had to live out what I had taught others. As I faced the pain of rebuilding my life, I used those moments to reflect and examine where God was leading me. Right in the midst of my grief, when I felt shattered and unsure of what lay ahead, God gave me an assignment: He instructed me to write my first book, *That Was Then, This Is Now: This Broken Vessel Restored*, which tells the story of my journey. I had no idea how to write a book, nor did I know anyone who could guide me through the publishing process. But I said yes, trusting God would lead the way.

By that time, I had undergone a deep healing and restoration process. I was finally ready to share my truth with the world. While I had been married, my life was content—co-pastoring in our local church, raising our children, and working my 9-to-5 job. That was all I knew, and I thought that was all I would ever do. But when life changed, I was forced to adjust and navigate an unfamiliar road. Yet, in the midst of that uncertainty, God had given me a word: "Write a book."

Though the path ahead was new, it was the one He had assigned for me. That road led me to discover parts of myself I never knew existed. It opened my eyes to a future full of possibilities—a future I hadn't dared to imagine. With each step, I realized that God's hand was still on me, but in a different way. He was preparing me for something greater, something beyond what I had known. It was through that journey that I found my voice—a voice that would reach millions, stir up creativity, and expand my influence in ministry.

As I ventured into this new chapter, I realized many people had stories inside them waiting to be told. Testimonies of God's miraculous work were left unwritten. They only needed someone to show them how to pull those words out. That became my assignment: to guide others in sharing their stories and glorifying God through their testimonies. I was still partnering with

God, but this time in a new way—outside the four walls of the church.

Looking back, I see how God was at work, even when everything seemed broken, scattered, and damaged. He was forming something beautiful out of my pain, giving me new visions, dreams, and insights that I never could have imagined. He opened doors I never would have been able to walk through on my own. Every step I've taken, every book I've written, and every life that has been touched was all because God wanted me to see that I could do it—I could rebuild my life, achieve my goals, and move forward without the bondage and scars that once tried to break me.

Those hard lessons pushed me to walk a new path, one that has allowed me to reach far beyond the confines of the church and into the lives of countless people. Today, I stand as a living testimony that even in the darkest times, God is working to birth something greater than we can ever imagine.

To those of you who may be walking through a season of heartbreak, loss, or uncertainty, I want to remind you that this is not the end of your story. I know the pain can feel overwhelming, and the road ahead may seem unclear, but let me assure you—God is still at work in your life. The pressure you're feeling, though painful, is shaping and preparing you for something greater. Your trials are not in vain. They are refining you, making you stronger, and birthing a purpose far beyond what you can see right now.

Jeremiah 29:11 (AMP)

'For I know the plans *and* thoughts that I have for you,' says the Lord, 'plans for peace *and* well-being and not for disaster, to give you a future and a hope.'

About the Author

Dr. Paulette Harper is an ordained pastor in the Gospel, and a nineteen-time best-selling, two-time award-winning author. She is also the host of Now Faith Is TV. Paulette is the founder of Faith Business Success Virtual Summits, whose mission is to provide speakers with exposure and visibility to share their message globally. She is also a recipient of the 2024 RiseHer Presidential Lifetime Achievement Award and The Passion Purpose Peace Award presented by Her Excellency, Dr. Theresa A. Moseley.

As the founder and CEO of Harper Media and Coaching Academy, Paulette serves as a self-publishing coach to aspiring nonfiction authors. She specializes in coaching women how to build their brand, expand their influence, and publish a subject matter book that positions them as experts in their field.

Paulette's unparalleled knack for curating compelling anthologies sets her apart, while her role as a compassionate and dedicated creative story coach empowers aspiring authors to unlock their full potential. In addition to being a resilient survivor of emotional trauma, she has earned a well-deserved certification as a Mental Health Coach.

Paulette invites you to connect with her for spiritual support, prayer, or if you're looking for a speaker for your church or conference. If you're also ready to take the next step and write your book, she is here to guide you on that journey as well.

Connect with Dr. Harper:

Social Tap: https://sociatap.com/drpauletteharper

My Transformational Leadership Journey

Dr. Theresa A. Moseley

Growing up in the 1960s, I saw women in the roles of teachers, nurses, secretaries, and homemakers. When I was in first grade, I loved the way my teacher led her class. She gave everyone an opportunity to respond and made every student feel special. I was a curious child—and wondered what I would lead one day.

My dad was in the Army, and he was my best friend. I wanted to be like him. As an Airborne Ranger, he was strong and wise yet gentle and kind. As a result, I joined the Army when I graduated from high school. My guidance counselor was disappointed with me. "You have a high-grade point average; you need to go to college!" My plan was to go to college after the military and use the GI Bill to help pay for college.

Enlisting in the Army was a great first step on my journey to being a leader and in learning to develop leaders. During my time in the military, I learned the importance of teamwork and collaboration. A collective effort in a group is just as essential as individual achievement. I learned the importance of discipline and accountability. Always holding yourself and your peers accountable is a crucial and effective leadership trait. I learned how to work under pressure and to adapt to changes.

One of the most important leadership skills I learned was clear communication. In the military, this could mean a life-or-death situation. I developed many other skills in the military and by watching my dad: empathy, compassion, and integrity. My military background laid the foundation for my future as a transformational leader.

My journey in the military came with challenges. I was only 18 when I joined and I was very small in stature. I only weighed 105 pounds, so I was perceived as weak by some who did not know me. Despite my age and size, I proved early-on in Basic Training that I was a strong person with leadership ability.

On the very first day, the drill sergeant told the 40 ladies in our company we had to build 40 wardrobes in eight hours before we could receive the rest of our gear. When the drill sergeant left, I told the ladies we could get this done in half the time. I asked who was good with directions. One lady said, "Oh, I can just look at the picture and tell you where everything goes." I said, "Okay we need three more just like her." The smaller ladies like me handled the supplies.

We completed the task in three-and-a-half hours. When the drill sergeant came back, he asked how we finished so fast. One lady said, "Baby Moseley gave us roles and responsibilities based on our strengths!" I immediately stood up and said it was a team effort. I did not want to take responsibility for what the team did together.

During the eight weeks in basic training, I was one of the fastest runners, the first person over the obstacle course, and I aced putting a weapon together in three minutes. The ladies saw that I was not weak, but strong–and committed to being a great leader.

When I ETS (End Term Service) from the military, I went to college and worked full-time. My personal growth continued. My time management skills assisted me in staying on task with my schoolwork as well as reporting to work every day on time. After I finished my Bachelor of Arts Degree in Speech and Theatre, I decided to go back to college and complete my Master's Degree in Guidance and Counseling and Doctor of Philosophy Degree in Education Administration. The course work in counseling theory and practice and leadership courses in both degrees contributed to my foundational knowledge and conventional wisdom in the field of counseling. I was hired by a school system and worked with them for 28 years.

My first job in the school system was as a high school guidance counselor. On my very first day, the principal asked me to provide professional development on how to communicate effectively with parents. I was honored to be chosen for this task. I loved working with the students, parents, teachers, and my peers. I learned how to problem-solve and how to be creative in solutions to problems.

One day, I heard the principal call the names of three students. Almost every day for a week, these students were told to report to her office. I wondered what was happening with them. One day, I asked the principal if I could help. She informed me the students were acting out in class and the teacher asked for assistance. I told the principal to allow me to work with the three young men. The first day I met with them in group counseling, and they told me they thought the class was a conceptual physics class; one where they needed to understand concepts and principles as opposed to mathematical equations. However, it was an algebra-based physics class which included math equations. Since the students did not understand how to solve the math equations, they acted out in class so they would not have to participate. Their teacher did not catch on to what was happening.

I had the perfect solution. I asked the students to stay after school with me, and I would have an algebra teacher teach them how to solve equations related to their physics class. We created goals during our first meeting; the first goal was to stay in class and behave. Another goal was to attack the problem at hand: ask questions if you don't understand something. We talked about always being on time and being respectful to classmates. I let the teacher know the students would be ready for participation soon; however, I asked her not to call on them until they were better prepared to answer correctly.

The algebra teacher and I worked with the students for six weeks and finally, they were comfortable with solving equations in class. After our tutoring and work on the affective and cognitive domain of these students, they were the best students in the class. The teacher could not believe the change in the work ethic and attitude of the students who used to cause so many problems.

Together, the algebra teacher and I used our leadership skills of empathy, creativity, and collaboration to solve the problem. I continued to build my leadership skills through my promotion to School Improvement Specialist. I worked with ten schools to develop and monitor their school improvement plans. Active listening was essential for the specialist, as we came from the central office and assisted the schools. Teamwork, trust, mutual respect, and competence were the keys to our success.

I was promoted to assistant principal and finally high school principal with over 1,200 students, 125 staff members, and over 2,400 parents and guardians. One of the most impactful things I did in my first year as leader was to create a vision, mission, core values, and beliefs with the staff. As a new principal, I did not want to come in and immediately change the program. I wanted to listen, learn, and make decisions together about what was in the best interest of our students and community. I found that when all stakeholders are involved in decision-making, they are more accountable for the results.

The Office of Professional Development was one of the best I ever worked with. Each year, we read new books including *Trust Matters*, *Leverage Leadership*, *Leadership and Self Deception*, *The Anatomy of Peace*, Biased by Jennifer L. Eberhardt, *Hacking School Discipline*, and *Great By Choice*. My personal library was filled with new reading material, which included books by Bernard Bass. I adopted the tenets of Transformational Leadership and used Idealized Influence, Individual Consideration, Intellectual Stimulation, and Inspirational Motivation to drive our instructional program. We also had our own professional development calendar based on the needs of our school. The goals were aligned with the information we received during "learning walks" in the school building. Each month during faculty meetings, we addressed our school vision and mission while triangulating data to determine the next steps. The skills I learned as a high school principal prepared me to run my own business after I retired.

During my time as an educator, I won three major awards and several proclamations from local politicians: Prince George's County Chamber of Commerce Outstanding Educator Award, Prince George's County Schools Outstanding Educator, and The State of Maryland EGATE Talented and Gifted Educator. I received a proclamation from the former county executive, the late Wayne Curry. In my first year as high school principal, our school was seen on NBC for the most improved truancy in the county. My years as an educator were some of the most fulfilling of my career.

During the pandemic, I created TAM Creating Ambassadors of Peace LLC. I started writing books on passion, purpose, and peace. One of the main reasons I started my business was to train schools and organizations how to have a peaceful climate. There is too much violence in the world and the workplace. I lost two students to violence during my first two years as a high school principal and three cousins to gun violence, so I was determined to develop a creed for peace, to speak and write messages to the world on what we can all do to make this world a better place to live—with no violence.

I was also determined to train leaders how to create a peaceful climate using transformational leadership techniques. Effective leadership is crucial as a positive work environment is essential for positive outcomes on the job. I also wanted to assist individuals in finding their divine assignment so they could become successful, fulfilled, prosperous, and have inner peace.

I had one book in 2014—and now I have 24. I've spoken all over the world in places like Troy, Michigan, New York City, Paris, and London. I speak on the importance of effective leadership, how to become an ambassador of peace, and living in your purpose. I am a Word of Life Ministries United Nations Peace Ambassador and I attend annual conferences in Geneva, Switzerland for training. My annual *Passion Purpose Peace Summit* is live and virtual to reach the masses. *The Essential Soft Skills for Effective Leadership – Steps to Leading with Grace* is my signature leadership book. In it, 24 experts on soft skills wrote chapters with case studies, practical strategies, and reflective questions. My book is an excellent training tool to build transformational leaders.

As I reflect on my leadership journey, I realize I had leadership skills before I entered the military. Some of the skills I have are innate. I was born with specific abilities which I developed over time through different experiences, jobs, and interactions with others. I've learned the importance of empathy, integrity, creativity, organization, problem-solving, time management, emotional intelligence, communication, collaboration, and adaptability.

Kobe Bryant said, "The biggest mistake we make in life is thinking that we just have time." Now is the time to lead your family, your staff, your community, and your friends to become productive citizens; to live in their purpose, to become successful, fulfilled, prosperous, and have inner peace. This will lead to peace at work, in the community, and in the home.

About the Author

Her Excellency Dr. Theresa A. Moseley is a United Nations Peace Ambassador, United States Army Veteran, International Motivational Speaker, 18-time Best-Selling Author, and 4-time International Best-Selling Author. She is also a three-time Award-Winning Educator who retired from education after 28 years of service.

Dr. Moseley has been featured in several magazines, including the cover of International Face Magazine, Women of Dignity, Speakers Magazine, Tap-In, Vision and Purpose Magazine, and The Black Family Magazine. She has also been featured in over 300 news articles worldwide. H.E. Dr. Moseley is the 2024 Women of Heart Global International Brand Ambassador.

H.E. Dr. Moseley is the owner and Chief Executive Officer of TAM Creating Ambassadors of Peace LLC. Her company provides inspirational and motivational speeches to groups looking for ways to resolve conflicts in the community, schools, and other organizations wanting to create a peaceful climate and culture. H.E. Dr. Moseley also provides professional development on the subject of Transformational Leadership.

H.E. Dr. Moseley uses her life experiences to address thought-provoking questions about finding one's purpose in life and finding your authentic self and is very forthright regarding everyone taking responsibility for creating a peaceful world. Dr. Moseley annually holds a three-day virtual Passion Purpose Peace Summit to promote world peace and purpose.

Connect with Dr. Moseley:

https://www.creatingambassadorsofpeace.com

Empowered to Lead and Live: My Aunt's Legacy in My Leadership

Cherise Buchanan

Do you remember the first time you recognized yourself as a leader? For me, it was during kindergarten, when our class set up an ice cream store. Somehow, I ended up being the manager. I don't recall exactly how that was decided—but even at that young age, I had a sense that I would have leadership roles throughout my life. I even "dressed the part," ensuring I looked like someone in charge. The memory feels like a foreshadowing of the leader I would grow into over time.

That early moment was just the beginning of my leadership journey. As I grew, I often found myself stepping into various leadership roles, formal and informal, whether in school projects, church activities, or family gatherings. It was as though leadership was a part of me. While these roles felt natural, I quickly realized that leading wasn't just about managing others—it came with responsibility, challenges, and, at times, the pressure to always be "on."

A Lineage of Strong Women

I come from a lineage of strong women, and I know their influence played a significant role in shaping who I am today. My mother was my first example of what it looked like to be a leader. Her husband (my father) passed away suddenly, which left her to be a single mother of two. Thankfully she had my other role model, my aunt, who assisted in raising me.

My mother and aunt had leadership roles within our church, their places of employment, and the community—all in addition to the leadership roles they carried in our family. From a young age, I watched as they navigated life with grace, resilience, and determination, even when resources were scarce. They showed me that leadership is about showing up, even when it's difficult, and that it's rooted in serving others.

It wasn't just their titles or the positions they held that astonished me—it was their actions. They took charge in every situation, made tough decisions, and always ensured things were done. Whether leading community events, organizing church functions, or simply being the glue that held our family together, my mother and aunt did it all. To me, they were like superheroes—capable of handling anything that came their way, all while keeping the needs of others at the forefront.

I was immersed in their world from an early age—attending meetings, conferences, and volunteer events. They embodied hard work, resilience, and a deep commitment to helping others. Despite full-time jobs and further education, they never stopped. I often wondered, "How do they do it all?" Now, people ask me the same question.

The Power of Example

My mother and aunt never gave formal lessons on leadership, but I learned by watching them. They showed me that true leadership is about empathy, compassion, and integrity. They took on unwanted tasks, spoke up when others were silent, and always cared for those around them. Their actions deeply influenced the leader I aspired to be.

I gleaned from their example that the importance of community and collaboration significantly impact one's leadership. As they modeled it, leadership could not always be a solo endeavor. It was about bringing people together, building relationships, and working collectively toward a common goal. They were never afraid to roll up their sleeves and do the hard work themselves—but they also understood the value of teamwork. These early lessons stayed with me as I grew into my own leadership roles.

The Cost of Leadership

Yet, as I got older, I started to notice something else about the leadership I had witnessed growing up. My mother and aunt worked tirelessly, often at the expense of their own well-being. They were constantly giving—of their time, energy, and even their resources. It didn't matter if they were tired, sick, or dealing with personal struggles—they kept pushing forward because they felt a deep sense of responsibility to others.

Looking back, I realize their selflessness, though admirable, came at a cost. They were always available, constantly helping others—but never practicing what we now call 'self-care.' Even vacations were interrupted by work. I often wondered, is this what leadership looks like—giving so much of yourself?

My Own Path to Leadership

As I stepped into adulthood, I found myself following in their footsteps. I, too, took on leadership roles in my community, within my family, church, and at work. To be a good leader, I thought I had to be "super" and wear my cape proudly. I worked long hours, volunteered for projects, and rarely said no, even when I knew I should. I believed leadership meant sacrifice, and I was more than willing to sacrifice my needs if it meant getting the job done.

One of my most vivid memories of this period is when I worked for a non-profit organization in my early 20s. I was incredibly sick—most likely with the flu—but I went to work anyway. I felt it was my responsibility to be there, to make sure things got done. No one had asked me to come in, but I had internalized the belief that leaders don't take unscheduled breaks. I spent the day pushing through the illness, running to the bathroom or nearest trash can to vomit, and forcing myself to complete certain tasks. There came a point when I was utterly drained, and finally went home early.

A Shift in Perspective

I experienced my aunt's passing firsthand. I watched my aunt, a pillar of strength in our family and community, whom I loved and admired deeply, take her very last breath--and it changed me.

My aunt, the essence of strength and resilience, rarely took time for her own needs. Experiencing her passing became a catalyst for change in my life. I finally recognized the value of self-care and the importance of my own needs.

I went to collect her things from her place of employment. They handed me one box of belongings. That box represented the entirety of my aunt's years of employment. This reality showed me that I could not continue operating as I had been. How could I continue to lead if I was burning myself out? More importantly, how could I be effective if I wasn't taking care of myself? When my aunt passed, it was a stark reminder of how short life can be and how, while you can work hard and be there for others, at some point your time will come and they will learn to live without you. It is important to *live*—not just to lead.

As my aunt and I were roommates, we would sit and have conversations every evening. Every evening we would sit and have conversations as we were roommates. I remember one of the last conversations we had before she passed. She told me, "Cherise, live your life.

Don't be like me; live your life." At the time, I didn't fully grasp what she meant. After all, she had lived a full life, hadn't she? She had accomplished so much, impacted so many people. But over time, her words began to resonate with me on a deeper level.

My aunt wasn't telling me to abandon leadership or to stop helping others. What she was saying was that life is more than just fulfilling duties. It's about finding joy, pursuing passions, and taking care of yourself along the way. Her message was clear: leadership is paramount—but it shouldn't come at the cost of your own well-being.

Helping Other Women Rise

As I forged my own path as a leader, I discovered a deep passion for helping other women step into leadership roles. Having strong female role models like my aunt and mother inspired me, and I wanted to leave that same legacy for my sister, nieces—and everyone I encountered.

I became committed to creating spaces where women could support and grow together—whether through organizing events, leading workshops, or mentoring. Like my aunt and mother, many women pour themselves into others without investing in their own well-being. I watched my mother and aunt lead, but often at the cost of their joy. I wanted to change that. I began developing programs that focused on both leadership and self-care, helping women understand they could lead without sacrificing their own needs. My goal was to show them they didn't have to choose between being a leader and living a fulfilling life—they could have both.

The C4 Method

As I began to internalize my aunt's message, I developed what I now call the "C4 Method," which encompasses Clarity, Courage, Communication, and Connection. This method helped me redefine my life and leadership in a way that prioritizes both service and self-care and allows me to get to the 5th C: **Confidence**.

- **Clarity**: I gained a clear understanding of who I was outside of the roles I held and what I desired for my life. Leadership wasn't my identity; it was a part of what I did, but not the whole of who I was.

- **Courage**: I learned to face my fears and to say no when necessary. I embraced the courage to lead in a way that honored my responsibilities and personal boundaries.

- **Communication**: I began to communicate my needs and desires more effectively in my personal and professional life. This allowed me to create space for myself without feeling guilty.

- **Connection**: I sought relationships and collaborations that aligned with my purpose and supported my growth.

This shift in mindset has allowed me to live more fully. I no longer wear the "superwoman" cape, and I'm okay with asking for help, delegating tasks, and prioritizing rest. As my aunt's words echo in my mind, I remind myself daily to live my life, to lead in a way that doesn't deplete me, and to create space for joy, adventure, and personal fulfillment.

I've had the privilege of helping others make transformative shifts in their lives, guiding them toward a life of flow, where they can confidently and unapologetically embrace their true selves. My passion for leadership has not only allowed me to manage high-performing teams in my professional career, but also build a coaching business that empowers women and creates lasting, meaningful impact.

Here is a beautiful client testimony from our time together:

"Cherise has been a great asset to work with as a support person as well as her business knowledge. Her presence and her confidence and the way that she speaks makes you feel like you can do it all because she speaks with comfort confidence and she's very concise with her and so I'm very thankful to have been able to work with her"

Living My Life

Today, I continue to lead–but I do so with a greater sense of flow and purpose. I continue to grow in my process of living a life that nourishes my soul. I've even been able to help my mother on her self-care journey.

Through starting my business, moving to a new city and recently a new state, and being okay to pause and do what is needed for me, I believe I am living a life my aunt would be proud of. I've learned that leadership isn't just about what you do for others; it's also about how you lead yourself. And part of leading yourself is ensuring that you're not running on empty.

As I reflect on my aunt's legacy, I'm grateful for the lessons she imparted to me through her actions and her words. Her strength and dedication inspired me to become the leader I am today. But her final lesson about truly living is the one that has made the most profound impact on my life.

So, I'll leave you with the same question my aunt left me: *How will you live your life?*

About the Author

Cherise Buchanan is the dynamic force behind *Rise & Shine 6012*, dedicated to empowering professional and businesswomen to rediscover their confidence, elevate their personal brand, and achieve financial success. Through her transformative *C Her Rise* coaching program and public speaking, Cherise equips clients with the tools to shine unapologetically. She also partners with organizations to ensure their stakeholders achieve meaningful, sustainable outcomes.

A committed leader with a passion for positive change, Cherise's influence extends beyond organizations, impacting individuals and communities. She infuses creativity, fun, and energy into every atmosphere, making each experience memorable. Cherise believes in recognizing each person's unique needs and works diligently to ensure everyone she interacts with feels seen and supported in their journey to the next level.

With over 20 years of service in ministry, Cherise attributes her success to the grace of God, knowing none of this would be possible without His guidance. While changing the entire world may be out of reach, she believes in the power of impacting one life at a time. Her mantra, "Let's Rise Together! There is room for all of us at the top," encapsulates her mission to inspire others to rise and shine.

Connect with Cherise:

- Free Resource - bit.ly/confidencehacks
- Instagram - @cherisebuchanan_c_her_rise
- Free Facebook Community - https://www.facebook.com/share/g/JFTcdqNhunh1Lqom/

From Home to the C-Suite: How Networking Drove Success

Susana Sarvis

Transitioning from a stay-at-home mom to the president of a company may seem like an unlikely path, but it's one that has taught me invaluable lessons about the power of connection. Networking, often reduced to exchanging business cards or sending a few LinkedIn requests, is so much more than a necessary activity. For me, it was the critical lifeline that propelled me from managing a household to managing teams, clients, and ultimately—an entire company. Throughout my career, networking has been a cornerstone of my success.

When I decided to re-enter the workforce, my path was far from clear. I had spent a few years as a stay-at-home mom, focusing on raising my twin boys and running our household. While this period of my life was immensely rewarding, there came a point when I knew I was ready for a new challenge. The question was how to leap from full-time motherhood back into the professional world. The prospect seemed daunting—after all, I had been away from the traditional workforce for years. But I also knew that I had untapped potential, and I was determined to reignite my career.

My first step back into the non-teaching workforce was in real estate, a field I had dabbled in before my hiatus. To get started, it was necessary to reconnect with people from my past—colleagues, mentors, and acquaintances who could help me navigate this new chapter. In the early days of my transition, I reached out to former co-workers, asking for advice and guidance. At first, this felt intimidating. After all, I hadn't spoken to many of them in years. The people I reached out to were not just polite; they were genuinely happy to reconnect. In many cases, they provided valuable advice or pointed me toward opportunities I wouldn't have known about otherwise.

This experience taught me one of the most valuable lessons about networking: never underestimate the importance of maintaining connections, even when you're not in the workforce. Treat this database like your client database. Have a systematic way to follow up with key contacts on a routine basis. Paramount to me, I never wanted to reach out "only" when I needed something. I wanted the relationship to be well-nourished, without a request or ulterior motive. Relationships that may seem dormant can often spring back to life when you need them most—but I believe cultivating a relationship without a need must be the primary goal of maintaining any business related relationship.

Rekindle Old Connections

As I navigated my new career, one strategy became increasingly clear: the power of rekindling old connections. Reaching out to past colleagues and acquaintances opened doors I hadn't even considered.

As I began working, initially part-time, in real estate, I quickly realized the field offered ample opportunities for networking. Real estate, at its core, is a relationship-based industry. My experience as a former teacher, where communication and empathy were crucial, served me well in this new environment. I found that my ability to genuinely connect with others set me apart. While real estate can be competitive, I discovered collaboration and building strong relationships were often more valuable than competing.

Networking in real estate wasn't just about attending industry conferences or formal business events—it happened everywhere. In fact, one of the most significant networking moments in my career happened during a casual double date. My former husband and I were invited to dinner by his work customer, and the wife of the host turned out to be an employee at a real estate firm. What started as a casual conversation over dinner turned into a pivotal career opportunity with her encouraging me to interview for an opening with her brokerage employer. Soon after that dinner, I interviewed with the company, and was offered a different job than I initially applied for at that real estate firm. My career took off from there.

This taught me a vital networking truth: take advantage of every opportunity!

If you've been out of the workforce for a while, don't hesitate to reach out to former colleagues or mentors. A simple message asking how they're doing can lead to meaningful conversations about your career aspirations. Even if years have passed, people are often happy to reconnect and support your next steps.

You never know when a casual interaction may lead to something bigger. Whether it's a local community event, a coffee date with a friend, or a more formal networking session—be sure to keep an open mind. Be present, introduce yourself to new people, and look for ways to create genuine connections. It's often in these unexpected moments that the most valuable opportunities arise.

Balancing the demands of work and family was one of my biggest challenges during this transition. Networking can be time-consuming, and as a mother, time was something I didn't always have in abundance. However, I quickly realized that networking doesn't have to be about attending every event or shaking every hand in the room. What matters most is intentionality. Rather than spreading myself thin, I focused on making the most of the opportunities I did have.

Be Intentional with Your Time

Rather than attend every networking event that came my way, I began to prioritize quality over quantity. I focused on the gatherings and conferences that aligned with my professional goals and offered the most value. Nurturing relationships, rather than making fleeting connections, became my focus. Follow-up was critical—after meeting someone, I'd send a quick email or connect on LinkedIn, helping me stay top of mind and deepen those connections.

Especially when balancing work and family, it's essential to focus on the events and connections that align with your long-term goals. A smaller network of deep, meaningful relationships is far more valuable than a large network of shallow connections. Being selective about investing your time and energy will help you build a strong, supportive network–without overwhelming yourself.

As my career progressed and I moved into leadership roles, the nature of my networking evolved. Now, I wasn't just connecting with peers—I was connecting with potential clients, business partners, and decision-makers who could influence the trajectory of my career. At this stage, networking became more than just a tool for career advancement; it was a strategic endeavor that allowed me to build influence and expand my professional reach.

Build a Network of Advocates

One of the most pivotal moments in my leadership journey came when an agent went out of her way to advocate for me. She made a phone call to a hiring manager at a major real estate firm on my behalf, vouching for my qualifications and potential. That one phone call changed the course of my career and led to a leadership role I had long aspired to. I had crossed paths with this hiring manager previously and, when the agent mentioned my name, the hiring manager recognized it immediately and asked for my resume to be emailed to him.

This experience highlighted a critical lesson: *your network can be your biggest advocate.* Building a network of advocates means fostering relationships based on trust, mutual respect, and shared values. When you take the time to build authentic, mutually beneficial relationships, your network will often return the favor in unexpected ways. People who believe in your potential will champion your success–sometimes without you even realizing it.

Networking isn't just about expanding your list of contacts—it's about cultivating relationships with people who are willing to advocate for you, whether by making a phone call, offering a recommendation, or connecting you with key decision-makers.

Another important lesson I've learned throughout my career is that networking isn't just about advancing your own success—it's also about lifting others up. As I transitioned into leadership roles, I made it a priority to mentor other women, especially working mothers who were navigating the same challenges I had faced. Helping others through networking, offering guidance, and making introductions became a source of fulfillment for me. There is something profoundly rewarding about helping others achieve their career goals through the power of connection.

As I reflect on my journey from stay-at-home mom to president, I can confidently say networking has been the single most powerful tool in my career development. Each step along the way was influenced by the relationships I nurtured, the connections I made, and the advocates who supported me. From reaching out to former colleagues during my initial career shift to building influence as a leader, networking has been the common thread that has tied my professional experiences together.

But perhaps the most important lesson I've learned is that networking is not a one-time event—it's an ongoing process that evolves with you. Whether you're just starting out in your career or you're well into your professional journey, the importance of networking never fades. In fact, it becomes even more critical as you take on new challenges and move into leadership roles. To advance, you have to know more leaders at other companies or within your own; that does not happen overnight. Networking is a "crockpot" versus a "microwave." Much like trust cannot be built overnight, neither can a strong networking relationship.

Networking isn't about collecting business cards, attending as many events as possible, or LinkedIn connections—it's about building meaningful, lasting relationships to help you grow, both personally and professionally. It's about creating a community of advocates who will support you, challenge you, and celebrate your successes. And it's about being intentional with your time, seizing every opportunity, and leading with authenticity and empathy.

My journey from stay-at-home mom to president has been filled with challenges, growth, and valuable lessons. But if there's one key to my success, it's the power of networking. It's not just a tool for career advancement—it's the foundation of leadership success. Whether you're re-entering the workforce, climbing the corporate ladder, or stepping into leadership, networking will be the key that unlocks your potential and opens doors to new opportunities.

So take the time to invest in your network—you never know where your next connection might lead.

About the Author

Susana "Su" Sarvis is an innovative leader who transitioned from stay-at-home mom to president of a real estate company. Su's career has been shaped by resilience, ambition, and a talent for building connections. With a background in education, her strong communication skills naturally led Su into training and coaching real estate agents, where she quickly rose to leadership positions. She is a real estate coach and the author of Texas Real Estate Commission Real Estate team courses.

As president of Realty Associates, overseeing over 1,200 agents across six offices, Su's leadership is grounded in empathy, collaboration, and a deep commitment to helping others thrive. Additionally, Su has authored influential real estate courses and is a passionate advocate for empowering women in leadership roles.

Through strategic networking and her dedication to fostering team success, Su has become a sought-after mentor and advocate for women in real estate leadership, as well as a podcast host for the She Leads Real Estate Podcast. Her ability to create a positive and growth-oriented culture has earned her a reputation as a transformative force in the industry.

Connect with Susana:

SuSarvisCoaching.com

Instagram @susarviscoaching, or listen in to the She Leads Real Estate Podcast.

Empowered to Rise: Unlocking the Strength to Overcome and Thrive

Elizabeth Meigs

At 14, I was full of life, chasing dreams of becoming a country music star. But in an instant, a devastating car accident changed everything. I was left with a traumatic brain injury, teetering on the brink of death–with less than a 25% chance of survival. The first 72 hours were critical, and I was placed in a drug-induced coma to give my brain the best chance to heal.

After three weeks, with the first 24-30 hours being touch and go, I finally woke up. I was completely dependent on others, needing to relearn everything. My voice, which once defined me, was silenced. It took over six months before I could speak clearly again. Returning to school was even more challenging. I felt invisible, constantly judged and rejected. My friends had moved on; I was left behind, spiraling into despair. For over four years, I often wished I hadn't survived. I cried out to God, questioning why He did this to me.

In my darkest moments, I heard a voice in my heart saying, *"I have a plan for you. You can't stop. You have to keep going."* This was my turning point. I realized God wasn't punishing me—He was guiding me through it. Faith and belief became my lifelines, giving me strength to keep moving forward, even when I didn't know how or when things would improve–so I began to trust.

Have you ever felt like you couldn't break free from negativity? I often felt that way. But I learned that the first step to breaking free was believing in a greater purpose. Every challenge I faced led me to where I am today, and I wouldn't change any of it. Each struggle brought me closer to my purpose.

Even though I had growing faith, my journey wasn't easy. Every night, I practiced gratitude, thanking God for my life and blessings and asking for guidance. This act became a powerful tool for managing stress and maintaining hope long before I understood its full impact. Science now supports what I discovered over two decades ago: gratitude helps with mental health, anxiety, and depression.

Jeremiah 29:11(NIV) says, *"For I know the plans I have for you,"* declares the Lord, *"plans to prosper you and not to harm you, plans to give you hope and a future."*

Trust in His promise, believe in the process, and keep moving forward.

Despite my imperfections, God never failed me. Through every trial, I learned that challenges make victory sweeter. By God's grace, I graduated high school with my class. I continued facing judgment in college, but eventually learned to let go of what didn't serve me. Those experiences helped me build strength and tap into the inner spirit of resilience that lies within us all.

After eight years and four changes in my major, I graduated with an associate's degree in Occupational Therapy. When I sat with my first patient, who had lost hope after a stroke, I shared my story. That's the moment I realized my brain injury was my superpower—it gave me the ability to connect with others who felt hopeless. My story became a bridge to inspire others to rebuild their lives.

When I became an Occupational Therapist, I felt confirmation that I was on the right path. From the beginning, I knew I had a purpose because God had told me, *"I have a plan for you."* I was eager to know what that plan was, but I had to learn to trust the process and make each day count.

After working in a rural rehabilitation unit for a year, the unit closed, and my hours were cut to part-time. I was disappointed because I had found purpose in working with stroke recovery patients. But I knew I had to keep moving forward. I picked up jobs in skilled nursing, home health, outpatient, and acute care. Over time, I became burnt out, constantly asking God why and seeking His guidance.

In May 2015, I faced a pivotal decision: move to Waco, TX, eight hours away from family, to return to the work I felt called to do—or stay in Kansas, burned out, living in a cycle of chaos and confusion. The decision wasn't easy, but I couldn't let fear stop me. I stepped out in faith and moved to Waco. Remember, fear is *False Evidence Appearing Real*. Often, fear is the very thing standing between you and your purpose. Stepping into the unknown felt daunting, but I trusted God's timing. That decision broke the cycle of burnout and confusion I was stuck in. Oftentimes, when we feel burnt out and overwhelmed, it's because we need to continue to move forward.

In July 2016, during an online lunch date, I was invited to a church in a nearby town, but I never went. A few months later, I moved to that same town and drove past the church often, being reminded of the invitation multiple times a week. After three months, I ran into the man who invited me, and that encounter stuck with me. I messaged him the next day, asking about church service times. He invited me to the second service and introduced me to his friends.

That Sunday, I met his friends, who would become like family. In the spring of 2017, I joined the church's Celebrate Recovery group and realized I could share my story with more people. I stepped onto the stage and shared how I had lived through depression and anxiety but found hope in God's healing. It was His voice of hope that kept me going.

One night, a woman approached me and said, *"Beth, I wasn't going to come tonight, but something told me I needed to be here. Now I know it was God—I needed to hear your story. It gives me so much hope."* That was the confirmation I needed to keep sharing, knowing my story could help others find light in their own darkness.

Two months after growing close to my group of friends, God spoke to me audibly. He said, *"I brought you and your friend together to bring you both closer to Me. You have to tell him this and tell him that you love him, and I love him."* I felt no fear, only peace. God also showed me my friend's heart and his potential to overcome his challenges. I felt a powerful love in that message as well; a love I didn't understand at the time.

The next evening, I shared God's message with my friend. He hugged me and said, *"I am so blessed to have met you, so happy I made you a part of my family, and I see the beautiful person you are."* His words strengthened my confidence in what God called me to do, though I didn't fully understand it then. I prayed for my friend daily and trusted God's plan.

In 2019, God introduced me to a natural plant medicine that helped me in ways I never thought possible after my brain injury. I began coaching others on its benefits, sharing what had helped me regain my life. This ignited a fire within me, as I knew God was calling me to help others, though I didn't yet fully understand how He would accomplish it. But as I started coaching clients to regain their lives, I began to see the power in what I was doing. A world of possibilities opened before me.

Later, I met a man I thought shared my faith, and in 2020, we married. I moved to the Dallas Fort Worth area, leaving behind my support system. After we married, I worked as an Occupational Therapist, mostly on weekends—which kept me from attending church. I joined networking groups during the week to promote my natural health solutions. I met business owners along the way who encouraged me to keep sharing my story. They were a blessing from God.

But as God opened doors, the enemy tried to close them. My husband often said, *"No one will ever pay you to tell your story. Your only financial security is through your degree."* But I knew better. God's voice was always stronger, and I held onto His promise that I would one day be on stage sharing how He worked through me. After all, that was the dream He had placed on my heart.

In February 2023, I learned about a two-day speaking conference that would give me a professional demo reel. I knew this was God opening a door. Despite my husband's objections, I participated in this event.

The seminar was held March 27-28, 2023. After my 6-minute speech, the leader said, *"This is where you were meant to be."* I received a standing ovation, and many said, *"You can't ever stop telling your story."* One man said, *"Your story needs to go nationwide—you can help so many people."* I knew I was on the right path; this was the confirmation I needed.

During the week of the speaking seminar, I also learned that my old friend, who invited me to church in 2016, asked how I was doing. With this message from a girlfriend, I sensed he was not in a good place. God had put my friend on my heart four months before this night. God's words flooded my heart again, *"I brought you two together to bring you both closer to me."*

On April 3rd, 2023, I received a call from the coach from the seminar, offering me a scholarship to his 4-month coaching program. That night, I shared the news with my husband—but his response was cold, saying, *"Until I see in writing that there are no fees, you're not allowed to do it."* When I began to cry, he looked at me with a look of pure hatred and asked, *"Why are you crying?"* I responded, *"Because this is who I am. This is what God has called me to do, and now that He's making a way, you're telling me I can't?"*

But I knew better. The coach had been moved to tears by my story, and for the past 2 ½ years, God had surrounded me with business owners who believed in me and offered their help. They lifted me up as I was being broken down at home.

That night before bed, I prayed, crying myself to sleep, asking God for clarity. On Wednesday, I received a sign from an old friend I hadn't seen in over four years, who said, *"If your husband doesn't support what God has called you to do, then God doesn't support your marriage."* That was the clarity I needed. My eyes were opened!

I called the Director of Therapy at my Dallas job and arranged a transfer to Waco. Within 24 hours, I was approved for an apartment in a safe neighborhood I could afford. My former dog groomer from Waco offered me a place to stay until I could move into my new apartment.

On Easter weekend 2023, my husband was playing piano at a church service, so I packed my essentials and left. At midnight on Easter morning, I arrived at my dog groomer's house in Waco. At that moment, the peace I had lost during my marriage finally returned.

Over the following months, I received more clarity than I had in years. I realized the strategies I had developed during my recovery were what had helped me survive my marriage. These strategies, developed 24 years ago through God's grace, are now backed by science for their benefits in managing mental health, anxiety, and depression. This is my 'why.' I created my *Pathway to PEACE Method*™ to help others build a strong foundation and tap into their inner spirit of resilience, just as I did.

You are no different from me. Each of us has a purpose, and everything you need to fulfill that purpose is already within you. The journey won't be easy, but by facing challenges head-on and refusing to give up, you can become stronger, more resilient, and step into your purpose. Let my story be proof that your breakthrough is possible.

Your pain has a purpose. My journey has shown me that with faith, gratitude, and resilience, you can turn your greatest challenges into your greatest strengths. When your struggles become your superpower, no one can take that away.

About the Author

Elizabeth Meigs is a passionate Transformational Coach, Inspirational Speaker, Author, and the Founder of Elizabeth Inspires. Through her signature Pathway to PEACE Method™, she empowers individuals to break free from the chains of confusion, overwhelm, and doubt, helping them pursue their God-given purpose with clarity and resilience.

Drawing from her personal journey of overcoming a traumatic brain injury and navigating life's challenges, Elizabeth provides practical, faith-based strategies to protect mental and emotional well-being while equipping others to thrive in every area of their lives.

Guided by the transformative power of hope, Elizabeth's mission is to help people embrace their calling and unlock their full potential. Through her coaching, courses, and speaking engagements, she offers the tools to build confidence, find inner strength, and create a life aligned with God's plan.

In appreciation for taking the time to read about how God has worked miracles in her life—and to demonstrate how He can do the same in yours—Elizabeth invites you to a FREE VIP 1:1 Pathway to PEACE Method™ Discovery Call. When you book today, you'll also receive the "Guide to Double Your P.E.A.C.E and Joy with the Pathway to Peace Method™, Guaranteed!*" Visit her website to start your journey from surviving to thriving.

Connect with Elizabeth:

elizabethinspires.com

FROM TRIALS TO TRIUMPH: MY JOURNEY OF RESILIENCE AND LEADERSHIP

DAWN STONE

My life's journey started as the child of a teen mother, who was no stranger to struggle and a host of challenges. In some ways, I grew up with my mother; she taught me how to ask questions, exercise my voice within, and take calculated risks to learn how to win. Ironically, my mother's voice was muted for most of her life—yet she found a way to help me excel despite her own pain and disappointments. Many of these experiences, though fraught with hardship, sowed the seeds of resilience and tenacity within me, qualities that would later define my leadership and drive my purpose.

From a young age, I was captivated by the concept of transformation. My desire to be liked and perfect created a hyper-focus on being the best I could possibly be, even at the tender age of six. After all, I wanted to be the best student and daughter I could possibly be. I recall my elementary school teachers calling me aggressive and tenacious as a student. "She doesn't need to be that here. She has time." What they didn't understand about my journey was that school was a way for me to escape and enjoy winning. It was the one place I was celebrated for what I knew and consistently given an opportunity to shine. I learned this academic habit from my mother, who had buried her own dreams in books and in me.

My journey into adulthood and the many transformations in my life reminded me of my elementary days in recess, as I searched every leaf for signs of life in the springtime. I enjoyed catching a glimpse of life as a butterfly emerged from its molten shell. These were early signs in my young life where I witnessed the greatness of God. And it led me to believe we all had the ability to change and improve at every stage of our life.

Watching caterpillars transform into butterflies, I became fascinated by the idea of personal metamorphosis and began to consider myself a monarch. As the butterfly, there were days when I found myself in situations that forced me to enter the cocoon to heal and rest. The beauty of this journey gave me time to reach a higher vibration so when I emerged, my wings were stronger and more beautiful than before. This is the power of God, shown through the life of one of the earth's smallest and most beautiful creations; the power to transform and renew through the challenges life brings.

A monarch butterfly is known for its endurance and navigational abilities, which exemplifies my entire life. Not only does it travel over 3,000 miles in the fall, the monarch butterfly also plays a crucial role as a pollinator in our ecosystem.

The monarch's display of interconnectedness and collaboration demonstrates how and why transformation is imperative for leaders. This belief—that no matter where we start, we all have the power to change our path—became central to how I approach both life and leadership. It carried me through the mountains and valleys of my life in addition to multiple life-threatening and transformative moments, each shaping and strengthening the leader I would become.

The Flight Begins

Stepping into Meigs Middle School, Nashville's very first academic magnet middle school, felt like embarking on a grand adventure. My near-perfect academic scores were quickly challenged after leaving my tight-knit black neighborhood for this new experience. The historic brick school building, with its tall windows and echoing hallways, welcomed me into a world brimming with both possibilities and fears. As an ambitious young Black girl with a head full of dreams, I carried more than just textbooks in my backpack—I carried the hopes and aspirations of my family and community, all of us believing education was the key to unlocking new doors.

The classrooms buzzed with energy, ideas fluttering around like monarch butterflies in a sunlit meadow. We tackled challenging problems and engaged in spirited debates that ignited a spark within me. Yet, amid the excitement of academic rigor, I was also navigating the uncharted waters of puberty. Being a quirky late bloomer with a love for languages and a smile that could fill a room, I often felt like a butterfly searching for her place among the flowers. I discovered that the social landscape was a bit of a maze, but realized I had to stay consistent even when afraid.

Those formative years at Meigs Middle School didn't just fill my mind with knowledge; they helped me discover the strength of my own wings. I learned that leadership isn't about fitting into someone else's mold, but about confidently embracing your own journey. By staying true to myself—celebrating my heritage, my quirks, and my passions—I began to inspire others to do the same. The very qualities that once made me feel out of place became the vibrant hues that defined my path.

During my twenties, I endured both physical and emotional challenges, including the birth of my first child as a single mother. The success I found in the classroom transferred to my career; however, I consistently failed in romantic relationships. This made me feel embarrassed and insecure, especially during my three perilous childbirths–all which literally almost ended my life with each delivery.

Each pregnancy tested my physical and emotional limits. Yet, through these trials, I drew profound strength from the women around me and the glimmer of hope that filled my heart as a mother. My children's eyes, filled with innocence and expectation, reminded me of my reasons to persevere. They anchored this monarch, fueling my resolve to overcome adversity and continue my flight.

The Winter Months

"Conflict chose me, I didn't choose it." I recite this quote often. I found comfort in it, especially after being downsized three times during my thirty-year career. This leg of the flight clipped my wings and bank accounts. It was incredibly heartbreaking because I spent over a decade building my career. With each downsizing, I had to rebuild my relationships, restore my confidence, and replace my bank account.

My first layoff was the catalyst for my first husband leaving our family and stating, "We weren't doing that well anyway," on the way out the door. While he received a promotion at work, I packed our home in California and returned to my mother's home, where I stayed for eleven years. This stretch of my flight taught me that when we are in the cocoon of life, healing and creating a rebirth helps us come back even stronger. I drew closer to God and was grateful that my mom—my first hero—took us in while I healed from the abuse, depression, and multiple losses.

I found the strength to rebuild again when my second marriage failed.

This time, I healed in my own home with the help of a licensed professional and daily prayers. However, I faced a challenge in 2021 that proved more dangerous than childbirth and the loss of my career: a stroke. Picture this: a healthy and active divorced mother of three, taking zero medication—before August 16, 2021. And then the stroke. I was hospitalized for a week, unable to walk, talk, or even dress myself. This was the ultimate challenge, and it tested my resilience to its core.

Suddenly transformed from a dynamic professional to a patient relearning basic skills, I confronted my vulnerabilities head-on. I used sign language to communicate several weeks after the debilitating experience and five months later, I was finally able to dress myself. This period taught me patience and the importance of acknowledging every small step forward. It also deepened my resolve to support others facing similar trials, underscoring my commitment to empathetic and compassionate leadership.

Emerging From The Cocoon

Divorce marked a pivotal chapter in my life, prompting a profound reevaluation of my identity and capabilities. I spent the first ten years of my professional career planning what I thought was the perfect set-up for my future husband. I completed two degrees, climbed the corporate ladder with a six-figure salary, and purchased assets in preparation for life as a financially responsible, morally abundant, and understanding spouse. What I found was a dream deferred while managing dual roles as a single mother and tenured professional challenged with proving myself, tackling workplace stereotypes, and managing my physical and mental health simultaneously. I often felt overwhelmed by the magnitude of my responsibilities and the demands of the workplace. Yet, this phase revealed my true resilience, teaching me that every ending heralds new beginnings. Over the years, I found that focusing on the things you can control is the best way to move forward in your life, regardless of your circumstances.

My professional journey spans six diverse industries, and each presented unique challenges—from overcoming skepticism and proving my worth to consistently battling to be seen, valued, and heard in spaces where I was often the only woman or person of color. These experiences not only tested my professional mettle, but also pushed me to confront and conquer the imposter syndrome lurking within.

During these times of self-doubt, I crafted a personal growth plan, which later became the foundation of my first book, *Positive Pudding: 30 Days to a More Positive You*. Writing this book allowed me to distill the essence of my experiences into actionable lessons on positivity, resilience, and growth—a guide for others navigating their own challenges. It was the first time I fully extended my wings without reservations. It felt so good knowing that my secrets, my flaws, my fears, and my disappointments were seen as colorful life lessons consisting of circles, lines, and triangles perfectly tattooed on my Monarch wings, unique to me yet art for the world to see. When you find ways to honor your butterfly journey, you ignite the power within, sometimes without even knowing.

Life As A Butterfly

The true measure of my leadership became clear when I began inspiring college students by sharing my story and igniting a sense of possibility in their lives. This initial engagement laid the foundation for my future role as the founder of *The Conflict Chick LLC*, where I now support thousands of individuals and organizations globally who seek guidance in personal development and conflict resolution.

The work I do has a lasting impact, not just on individuals, but on entire organizations and communities, reinforcing the importance of leading with purpose and compassion. Hearing the stories of students and leaders whose lives have transformed reminds me of the significance of my work and the power of leadership rooted in service. My experiences serve as maps for other monarch butterflies to follow on their journey.

This journey is a call to action for each of you to reflect on your own challenges and the lessons they've imparted. Each difficulty you've faced holds invaluable insights that can propel you and others forward. Remain committed to the path you are destined to walk, and let your personal and professional journeys be driven by purpose.

In my book *Seven Paths One Destination*, I explore the idea that while our paths may differ, our goals are aligned—to lead lives marked by purpose and impact. Embracing this perspective has empowered me and those I have had the privilege to lead.

As I close, remember this: *You are not defined by your past but refined by it.* No two monarchs have the same path, but they both share the 3,000-mile journey. When you build endurance in your mindset, it is the difference between giving up and digging in.

I have shared how digging in can propel you to your greatest accomplishments, even when you are the only one to see and believe it. Each challenge in life is a unique opportunity, an invitation to rise and evolve into the best version of yourself.

I ask you to stand firm in your truth, lead with authenticity, and never underestimate the transformative power of your own resilience. Your flight through life may be difficult at times, but your story could be the beacon that guides someone else to start their journey of change.

About the Author

Dawn Stone is a trailblazing conflict resolution expert, acclaimed keynote speaker, and certified Rule 31 mediator, with over three decades of experience transforming the leadership landscape. As the founder and CEO of *The Conflict Chick LLC,* Dawn has empowered thousands of leaders across corporate and nonprofit sectors worldwide through her dynamic strategic consulting and conflict coaching.

She is the author of *Positive Pudding,* co-author of *Seven Paths, One Destination,* and the visionary force behind the "Not Your Average Chick Summit" and "One Day Getaway," where she inspires working women to reclaim their strength and flourish both personally and professionally.

Dawn's unwavering resilience stems from overcoming formidable life challenges—rising from poverty, navigating loss, and triumphing over discrimination. Her transformative work in conflict resolution has revolutionized inclusive leadership, breaking barriers to foster emotionally healthy and engaged workplaces. Driven by her compelling story of perseverance, Dawn passionately advocates for authentic leadership, emotional intelligence, and meaningful employee engagement, inspiring others to harness their own strength and lead with impact.

Connect with Dawn:

www.theconflictchick.com

Leading with God, Passion, and Purpose
Dr. Iris Wright

I believe that leading properly requires God, passion, and purpose. Life's journeys often guide us to our purpose, and I've learned this truth the hard way. My story began when I was eighteen, during one of the darkest times in my life. I was falsely accused of a crime I didn't commit—the unthinkable accusation of abusing my own daughter.

It all began after breaking up with her father, a man I had known since junior high. We had a history and a deep connection, and I thought we would be together forever. I never imagined that ending our relationship would lead to such betrayal.

One day, I picked up my daughter from his family's house. When my daughter and I arrived home, she showed me painful sores between her legs. Worried, I immediately made an appointment with her doctor and rushed to Rite Aid to buy an oatmeal bath and Calamine lotion, desperate to soothe her discomfort.

The doctor diagnosed my daughter with impetigo, a common skin condition, and prescribed medication. I felt relieved—finally, an answer. Something I could handle. I asked her father to watch her while I went to work to arrange some time off.

A few hours later, I returned to her father's house, completely unprepared for what awaited me. The police were there. They told me I couldn't take my daughter. Shortly after, he was granted emergency custody.

At that moment, I still believed everything would work out. I had no reason to think otherwise. I cooperated fully with the authorities, trusting that the truth would clear my name. But my world shattered when I was arrested and faced with the possibility of spending over 20 years in prison– for something I didn't do. I couldn't comprehend what was happening. I had gone from a young mother doing her best to protect her child to being treated like a criminal.

For two agonizing years, I waited for my trial, living in constant fear and uncertainty. My name was dragged through the mud, my reputation destroyed. Worse still, I was separated from my daughter, my heart aching for her every single day. When she finally returned to me nearly five years later, I discovered she had contracted a sexually transmitted disease during her time apart from me. It was a blow that nearly broke me all over again. The people who were supposed to protect her had failed her in the worst way.

This life-altering experience unleashed a torrent of anger and hatred inside me. I felt betrayed by the people around me, by the justice system– and even by God. I found myself constantly in trouble, getting into fights and being arrested repeatedly. It was as if I no longer cared what happened to me. My lowest point came when I was incarcerated in a maximum security prison, and the judge threatened to take all of my children away from me. It was a wake-up call, but I still didn't understand how to move forward or release the rage that consumed me.

I thought God had forgotten about my daughter and me. I felt abandoned, lost, and hopeless. Why would He let something so horrible happen? Why would He let me suffer so much? I didn't realize then that God was still with me, even in the darkest moments. He was preparing me for something greater, something I couldn't see at the time.

It took me over two decades to begin healing. For years, I lived in survival mode—an exhausting, toxic place to be, both mentally and physically. I was always on edge, never allowing myself to rest or trust anyone. It's easy to get stuck in survival mode, to believe that's all life will ever be. But survival is not living. In 2017, a turning point came when the Governor granted me a pardon.

By 2018, my family and I moved to start fresh, away from the memories of the past. Moving away was an essential part of my healing. I needed to distance myself from the people and places that reminded me of all the pain I had endured. In a new city, I could breathe again. I could begin to dream about the future instead of constantly reliving the past.

In 2020, I took a leap of faith and became an entrepreneur, opening my first business. By 2022, I launched my home care company, Caring Hearts Telecare. This marked the moment when I realized I had to confront the wounds I thought were long-closed. I needed healing to move forward, especially as a leader responsible for others.

To truly heal, I first had to rebuild my relationship with God. I had to trust that He had a plan for me, even if I didn't understand it then. I learned to accept what had happened to me and my daughter, painful as it was. However, acceptance didn't mean I condoned the injustice—I had to forgive, not forget. It meant I could no longer allow my past to dictate my future. Next, I had to relearn how to love myself and forgive those who had hurt me. Forgiveness wasn't easy, but it was necessary for my peace. Finally, I discovered the power of writing. Picking up the pen became a major step in my healing journey. Writing allowed me to process my emotions, to make sense of everything I had been through. It became my therapy, my way of reclaiming my voice.

In 2023, I became a best-selling author. That same year, I went live on Facebook and shared my story publicly for the first time. The response was overwhelming. People reached out to share their own stories of injustice and pain. I realized then that my story wasn't just mine—it was a way to help others heal, too. Inspired, I decided to lead an anthology project called Injustice, where others could share their experiences and begin their own healing.

In June 2023, we launched the book *Injustice*, which became an Amazon bestseller. We held our first Injustice celebration, and the book is now featured in bookstores. In 2024, we published *Injustice Volume II*, which also became a bestseller and won the International Impact Award. Our books are now being used in Social Justice programs in colleges. We're preparing to launch *Injustice Volume III* and host an annual Injustice celebration. I've also been traveling and speaking on stages, receiving awards for my work in social justice.

Today, I advocate for others facing injustice. I'm currently helping with a clemency case to release a man who has been incarcerated for 27 years, serving an 80-year sentence. In August 2024, I began pre-law school—a path I had tried to walk many times before, but only now does it feel right. This journey is different; it feels fulfilling and rewarding. I'm finally walking in my purpose.

In the past few years, I have experienced peace I never thought possible. God has placed the right people in my life, those who align with my passion and purpose. I now only speak on stages that are purposeful and impactful. I've learned that authentic leadership comes from moving and leading with purpose.

Every action I take is driven by passion, purpose, and impact—not money. God has shown me that when I follow His plan, everything else–including financial success–will follow. Every year, my life continues to elevate, and I'm grateful I can help others rise as well. I never imagined that the very thing that once broke me would lead to my purpose.

The last few years of my life have been unforgettable, a rollercoaster of experiences that have shaped who I am today. I've learned that a strong, respectable leader leads with both passion and purpose. God has shown me that through faith, anything is possible.

> *"Leadership is about making others better as a result of your presence and making sure that impact lasts in your absence." – Sheryl Sandberg*

About the Author

Dr. Iris Wright is a dynamic serial entrepreneur, award-winning author, and advocate for innovation and community service. She is the visionary behind several successful ventures, including Caring Hearts Telecare, Caring Hearts Birthing Services, and the popular platform Real Talk with Iris.

Dr. Iris's entrepreneurial journey is marked by her commitment to improving lives through her diverse businesses. A pioneer in telehealth integration within home care, Iris has been instrumental in modernizing healthcare services. Her expertise was spotlighted during an influential seminar with Leading Age in July 2022. Iris's contributions have earned her numerous accolades, such as the Community Leader Award from ACHI Magazine and the Black Excellence Award.

AAuthor Iris Wright is celebrated for her bestselling book series, "Injustice," which has garnered international acclaim and several prestigious awards, including the 2024 International Impact Award. Iris was also recognized as one of The Book Profits Club's Top 20 Authors of the Year.

Beyond her professional achievements, Iris is devoted to her family. She has been happily married for 13 years and, together with her husband, they cherish their blended family of six children and three grandchildren.

Connect with Dr. Wright:

- Website: [iris-wright.com] (https://www.iris-wright.com/)
- Facebook: [Author Iris Wright] (https://www.facebook.com/authoririswright)
- Instagram: [@author_iris_wright] (https://www.instagram.com/author_iris_wright/)

The Whisper of Faith: From Desert to Destiny

Kristina S. Shauntee

In the tapestry of my journey, the threads of faith and leadership are intricately woven, reflecting the covenant I have embraced since my youth. From my beginnings as an assistant youth pastor in my twenties to co-pastoring alongside my husband today, every step has been guided by a profound sense of purpose and divine calling.

My journey into ministry began long before I ever stood behind a pulpit or held a Bible study. It started when I was just seven years old, in a moment so profound that it forever shaped the course of my life.

My mother had just made the heartbreaking decision to give me up to my grandmother, who would raise me. I was on a Greyhound bus, leaving Fresno, California, and heading toward Kentucky. As the bus rumbled through the dark desert, a heavy sadness and fear washed over me. The reality of abandonment settled in, and I stared out into the emptiness of the night, tears streaming down my face.

Wrapped in my white shawl, I tried to comfort myself—but the overwhelming weight of sadness was too much for my seven-year-old heart to bear. I remember clutching that shawl as if it were a lifeline, wishing I could make sense of the sudden changes in my world. But then, in an instant, something miraculous happened. That very shawl seemed to transform before my eyes, as if it had become the wings of an angel, gently enveloping me. In that moment, an overwhelming sense of peace and love surrounded me, like a gentle embrace from heaven itself. I heard a whisper, soft yet undeniable saying, "You are not alone. Everything is going to be alright."

I did not fully understand it then, but I now know that voice was God. He met me in my deepest despair and gave me something no earthly person could: the promise of His presence and the assurance I would never walk alone. From that moment, a faith was birthed in me, unexplainable yet unwavering, born from the depths of my sadness. That encounter planted a seed of trust in God, a trust that would carry me through countless valleys and mountaintops in the years to come.

As the years passed, that seed of faith took root and began to grow. My journey into ministry was not marked by a sudden, dramatic calling, but by a steady, gentle stirring within my spirit. Much like that whisper I had heard as a child, the call to proclaim God's Word was quiet but unmistakable. I could not shake the feeling that I was destined for something more—something that would not only change my life but impact the lives of others.

As a little acolyte at Walker Memorial United Methodist Church, I would sit in awe, watching my godfather, preach the Word of God with unapologetic boldness. Every movement and articulation captivated me; I studied him intently. On Saturday afternoons, I would dust the pews, dance around the sanctuary, pretend to preach my godfather, and help my godmother prepare the Sunday service programs. She was a model of grace—elegant, faithful, and dedicated to ministry and family, leading the choir and caring for her husband with the love of God radiating from her.

One Sunday, we had a guest woman pastor for the evening service. As she preached, it was as if a fiery glow surrounded her. In that moment, I knew deep in my heart that I, too, would one day proclaim God's Word. That whisper, which stirred within my spirit, was the beginning of my journey into ministry, urging me forward to preach the gospel and set the captives free.

In my early twenties, during my college years, the call of God on my life became unmistakably clear. I stepped into the role of assistant youth pastor at Buechel United Methodist Church, where my journey intertwined with two incredible mentors who had a profound impact on my spiritual and personal growth.

Their guidance was pivotal. They prayed with me, nurtured my spiritual growth, and constantly encouraged me to pursue excellence in my studies and walk with God. They reminded me not to shy away from my love for God or the undeniable calling on my life, urging me to embrace it fully. Through their mentorship, the path to my purpose became even more defined.

As a young woman, I embraced the role of assistant youth pastor with eagerness and humility, learning the intricacies of pastoral care and the transformative power of the Gospel. It was here, amidst the vibrant energy of youth and the challenges of nurturing spiritual growth, that I first glimpsed the depth of my calling. I was eager to serve, learn, and lead others toward the same peace I had experienced as a child.

Working with young people, I recognized the importance of faith in shaping their lives and futures. As I guided them through their own struggles, I often thought back to that moment on the bus, where God had met me so intimately in my pain. It was a reminder that God's presence is often most profound in the quiet, broken spaces of our lives—and it became the cornerstone of my ministry.

Over the past 27 years, my journey in ministry has been one of evolution, growth, and unwavering faith. What began as a calling in youth ministry expanded into a lifelong mission alongside my husband. Together, we were ordained and began serving as assistant pastors and directors of children's ministry at a megachurch in our hometown. During this time, we were also raising our two young sons, and I took on the incredible task of homeschooling them for 12 years. Today, they are both college graduates—young men who love God and walk confidently in their faith.

Those years of faith, family, ministry, and education were like walking through a fiery furnace— refining me as a wife, mother, church leader, educator, and humanitarian, with each role deeply rooted in purpose and growth. The trials were refining, a time of deep testing and strengthening of my faith.In that crucible of challenge, I learned to persevere, to truly walk by faith and not by sight. Forgiveness became a powerful lesson during this season, as I confronted painful moments that could have easily shattered me. Yet, those trials did not break me; they revealed who I truly was in Christ, refining me like pure gold.

Going through pain and hardship is never easy. Still, I have come to understand that it is often in those moments of profound struggle that we discover our true selves. Adversity has a way of exposing our strengths and our weaknesses, and through that revelation, we grow. Our faith is tested, our values challenged, and our priorities brought into sharp focus.

James 1:2-4 (KJV) reminds us of this truth: "My brethren, count it all joy when ye fall into divers' temptations; knowing this, that the trying of your faith worketh patience. But let patience have her perfect work, that ye may be perfect and entire, wanting nothing."

This process of being tested and refined is like the biblical metaphor of gold being purified by fire. Just as the fire removes impurities from gold, so trials purify our character and faith. I came out of that season of challenge not only as a stronger woman, but also more deeply committed to my calling and to God's purpose for my life. I made a resolute decision during those years:no matter what came my way, I would remain rooted and grounded in the love of God. I adopted discipline as my watchword, a steadfast commitment to infuse order and purpose into every facet of my existence as a woman, a wife, a mother, a pastor, and a leader.

As my husband and I transitioned into our roles as senior co-pastors, our union became a testimony to the beauty of shared vision and divine calling. Co-pastoring alongside my husband has been one of the greatest blessings of my life. Our ministry is not just a union of hearts but a collaboration that reflects the very essence of our purpose–to serve God's people with integrity, love, and compassion. Together, we navigate the complexities of leadership, always leaning on each other's strengths and seeking God's wisdom to guide us through every decision.

Our church has become a sanctuary where faith thrives, lives are transformed, and the love of God is tangibly felt in every corner. Finding my way as a woman called to preach and teach alongside my husband required deep surrender to the Holy Spirit's leading. I learned to walk in my calling while still supporting and submitting to my husband as the head of our family, honoring both our partnership in ministry and his role as my husband.

In addition to co-pastoring, I founded a homeschool enrichment program that served our community five days a week, tuition-free, with accredited and licensed teachers. This initiative was not just a ministry to my own children but a gift to families in our community, helping educate and nurture other people's children in a Christ-centered environment. The vision for this program was born out of my own experiences as a homeschooling mother, and it became another way for me to live out my calling to raise the next generation in both faith and knowledge.

Through the years, I have learned that leadership is not about the titles we carry or the platforms we stand on but about the lives we touch and the love we pour out. My journey as a woman called to preach, a pastor, and a leader has been marked by challenges—but it has also been a journey of deep fulfillment. It is through the fiery trials that I have found my purpose, and it is through God's grace that I continue to walk in it today. As I look back over these two decades, I am filled with gratitude for the journey; the refining, growth, and unwavering faith that has carried me through every season.

My story is one of covenant, faith, and purpose–fulfillment not just at the age of fifty, but throughout every stage of life as I continue to serve God, lead His people, and walk boldly in the calling He placed on my life years ago.

To the women who are called to preach, pastor, and minister: your calling is both divine and necessary. The world needs your voice, your heart, and your unique gifts to bring God's Word to those who need it most. As you step into this sacred role, remember you are equipped for the journey ahead. Challenges will come, but so will breakthroughs–and every step of obedience will yield fruit in God's perfect time.

My advice to you is this: never underestimate the power of preparation, prayer, and perseverance. Study the Word diligently, and lean into your relationship with God. Surround yourself with people who will uplift and encourage you. Ministry is not easy, but it is worth every sacrifice as you see lives transformed through your obedience to God.

Finally, take that leap of faith. Trust that God, who has called you, will also direct your steps. He has gone before you, and He will make a way even when it seems impossible.

WOMEN WHO LEAD

Lord, I pray for these mighty women of God, strengthen them, guide them, and fill them with Your peace as they answer Your call. In Jesus's name, Amen.

About the Author

Kristina S. Shauntee is a committed mentor with a heart for women called to preach, pastor's wives, and young women on the path to motherhood. Through her ministry, she provides encouragement, wisdom, and biblical support, helping women find purpose in their calling, whether in the pulpit, supporting their husbands in ministry, or stepping into motherhood with faith and confidence.

Guided by the foundational scriptures Proverbs 3:5-8 and Ephesians 3:14-21, Kristina lives out her roles as a wife, mother, pastor, mentor, and author with unwavering faith and love for God. She authored the transformative workbook "Faith-Driven Success Blueprint: Navigating Life and Business God's Way" and "Harvest and

Beyond," a faith-based journal. With a background in creative writing and theology, she excels as an executive copywriter, crafting compelling narratives for brands.

As a senior co-pastor at Courageous Faith Church alongside her husband, Kristina mentors individuals to overcome obstacles and fulfill their God-given purpose, her dynamic presence as a transformational speaker inspires audiences to embrace their calling with faith and determination. Kristina's life story embodies resilience, love, and the power of faith, leaving an indelible mark on all who cross her path.

Connect with Kristina:

http://www.kristinashauntee.com

Calling All Readers!

Have you been inspired by "*Women Who Lead*"?

Your voice matters, and we'd love to hear from you!

Share your thoughts, insights, and personal takeaways from the book by leaving a heartfelt review. Your review can help others discover the transformative power of faith and courage, and it means the world to us.

Here's how you can make a difference:

Visit the book's page on your favorite online retailer.

Leave an honest review sharing your thoughts, emotions, and the impact the book had on you.

Recommend "*Women Who Lead*" to your friends and family, encouraging them to join this inspiring journey.

Your reviews are a beacon of encouragement for both the authors and future readers, guiding them towards a life marked by courage and faith.

Thank you for being part of our community and for helping spread the message of hope, faith, and resilience. Your support means everything! #Womenwholeadreviews

Visionary Author Dr. Paulette Harper

www.pauletteharper.com

Thank you so much!!

OTHER BOOKS BY

DR. PAULETTE HARPER

Do you need a self-publishing coach?
Visit https://pauletteharper.com/services/

Solo Books

Fiction Inspirational

Secret Places Revealed (Award winner)
Living Separate Lives

Children

Princess Neveah: Lessons of Self Discovery

Nonfiction

That Was Then, This Is Now: This Broken Vessel Restored
Completely Whole
Faith For Every Mountain

Coloring Book

The Scriptures in Color

Anthologies (Nonfiction)

The Breaking Point
When Queens Rise
For Such a Time as This
I Survived The Storm
Resilience in Hard Times
Women who Soar
Arise From The Ashes
Breaking The Silence
Her Unbreakable Spirit
Women with Unshakable Faith

Write A Book With Me

Do you have a story you want to share?

Would you like to be in our next anthology?

WHAT'S IN IT FOR YOU?

- Instant credibility for writing a best-selling book
- Your personal worth will increase
- Speaking opportunities will open for you
- Your personal finance will increase
- Your personal brand will be connected with other like-minded people
- Notoriety – Your circle of influence will increase and be empowered

JOIN ME!

I want to personally invite you to partner with me and join the waitlist for the next anthology offered by Visionary Author Dr. Paulette Harper

Visit https://pauletteharper.com/opportunities to get on the waitlist for the next book collaboration.

Author Coaching Services

Offered by Dr. Paulette Harper

Join us at One Story University Online School.

Unlock The Writer In You 90 Day Program

One Story University is an online school that provides aspiring authors with a step-by-step process on how to write and publish their self-help, how to, and personal story books in 90 days.

Visit Unlock the Writer to get access to the course.

A group coaching program for coaches, speakers, thought leaders, and entrepreneurs who are ready to write, self- publish and launch a best- selling book in 90 days.

5 Module Outline

Module 1- The Story Framework: The purpose behind your book, getting clarity on your story and creating the outline is the foundation every writer needs in order to produce a great book. The best writers are those who can frame the outline of their content, ensuring each chapter flows consistently and concisely for the reader.

Module 2- Crafting Your Story: Writers must know their ideal audience so they craft content that compels, sells, and propels their readers. Creating a premise and promise statement assures you will achieve all three.

Module 3- Constructing Your Book: Putting your book all together requires knowing what goes in the front and back of your book, as well as, hiring the right literary team to help put your book together.

Module 4- The Publishing Lab: Now you're ready to learn the steps to finally publishing your book and securing your intellectual property.

Module 5 – Promoting Your Book: Before you can promote yourself and your book, you must establish a customized and focused marketing plan. Bringing a new book to the market will require a strategy, a vision and proper planning in order to generate book sales.

www.ingramcontent.com/pod-product-compliance
Lightning Source LLC
Chambersburg PA
CBHW071222160426
43196CB00012B/2376